Ghost Lights

Ghost Lights

poems by

Keith Montesano

Dream Horse Press
California

Library of Congress Cataloging-in-Publication Data:

Montesano, Keith 1981—
        Ghost Lights
                p.   cm

                ISBN 978-1-935716-00-6
                1. Poetry

10 9 8 7 6 5 4 3 2 1

First Edition

Cover: "Smoke Map" by Felicia Van Bork.
        www.feliciavanbork.com

Contents

Ghost Lights

I.

Before the Fires

This was before the fires, before boarded doors
and everyone clawing, before a way out, roads collapsing

into potholes, telephone poles snapped in half,
hanging by the last nerve. There was this man:

earrings and make-up stolen from his dead wife,
pink dress with white pumps clicking on the floor

of the East Side Dairy, where we rotted our teeth with candy
before grade school. We knew nothing of love and obsession,

madness or plain speech: the way his voice heightened
toward the pitch of hers, his fits of tears at the counter, palm

on a pack of Camels. There was the checkout girl glaring through
the man's eyes, trying to conjure her own future: her first

backseat groping, mansion and five children, anything but a soul
torn from the love of a man and his wife, something you could

actually see, maybe, through the smudged shadow and sweat
on the counter. And if you look now, something's there—

passing through, stopping to offer the difference
between the space of our world and the next: the sweet, stained

tongues of children, and those wrenched sobs of a man
who could never find his own way out.

Elegy Ending with Steve Reich's *Music for 18 Musicians*

I. Pulses (0:00 - 5:30)

First, a noose. Then the exhaust, fumes billowing
through the attic. You exit the garage, close the door.

Speakers all over the house. There's a clarinet
and you think the voice of just one woman.

Ten hours have passed; your wife's not coming back.
Repetition, staccato breathing, maybe more

than just one woman: the liner notes say four
(and all these years you never thought to look).

II. Section I – Section IV (5:30 - 27:30)

Today you will do it while the music is playing.
You recall the story of another husband who waited

and could bear it no longer, though the garage
was connected to the house, his wife and daughter

sleeping soundlessly upstairs. These women
are the Sirens, but where's the voice and marimba,

metallaphone and cello? Now the gas from the stove
as you refuse the pills, drugs she left in the cabinets

(only grabbing moisturizers, skin creams). You can't
tell a voice from a piano—tighten the noose

hanging from the chandelier, then loosen, light it on fire
in the backyard, early morning dew snuffing the flame.

Then you cut the ignition, as the garage is not
the ideal place. At 27 minutes in, you sprawl

on the kitchen floor, hiss of gas falling short
of heaven: those Sirens howling, muses

shedding clothes, your wife twenty years
before, the hill above St. Michael's graveyard,

cans of beer in both of your hands. There was
no full moon then—you couldn't see her body.

III. Section V – Pulses (27:30 - 67:00)

At age sixteen, your doctor told you, *Only marry if there will
be no divorce, talk it through, love should be a sealant.*

Now the pace quickens—pianos, metallaphone, voice—
and everything is percussion, unlike your slowing heart,

head on the only pillow she left. *And sex*, he said,
Make sure it's because of love; it can also be the cause.

Then you root through a drawer filled with tools,
find the electrical tape. It will be quicker

if the cracks are sealed: each window and door.
Now your breathing and the pulses slow

as the instruments and your own pulse blur.
You think Reich made the music for this—

remember again, it was winter, she was freezing.
Some snow covered the plots and graves below.

You held her hand, shivering. She told you
she was afraid, but you never asked her why.

Two Halves: Elegy for One Summer's Dawn

Bellefontaine: a town on the way to somewhere else, a place
where you run out of gas, stop to make love on a picnic table

somewhere by the wheat field—when, toward magic hour, the boy
has already loaded the gun, the smell of bacon wafting outside

his grandparents' house, where he goes to make their deaths real.
The news always first: yellow tape stretched over dirt roads,

clean white houses, scarred fields and blood spackling the earth.
Now the shouldered camera, microphone shoved toward the mouth

of the sheriff, who can't deal with this, but gives them
what he knows: tombs of two connected houses, six dead bodies,

no roses stuck between their teeth. Only silence through the fields
that morning, soybeans slowly curling to ash, faint pops

of gunshots and confusion, no note, no explanation, the day
before graduation. There's too much to figure out now: divorce

and reflux, scorned relatives within walking distance, feigned
forward planning before the battles with lawyers, splitting up

the land. Only the dog galloped through the neighboring field
that morning, the four of us parked in a gas station in a town

we didn't recognize, near waking or sleeping, the oil on our faces
we couldn't rub off or in, and the girl I knew in the backseat

only hours before we silently cast *Just once* and *Never again*
as the others stood inside for fat and sugar, bloodshot and reeling,

to tell themselves, *We're empty, will be well again.* And I remember
both of us loving others, never having before what we decided on then:

silent consent—ten minutes, maybe less—the time for the gun
aimed at their bodies, the deed carried out and no turning back.

Days of 1994

Before the pot smoke and broken lamps
    in Manassas, Virginia, I found Annie's letters
        under our high school football bleachers

during a game—abandoned, scribbled
    confessions to three friends on pink
        and white paper: her hopes and fears,

her longing for sweets at the grocery store,
    the problems with her boyfriend. I told
        no one, obsessed with her physique,

the gray sheen of her teeth, and how ribs
    snaked beneath her skin. I wanted to leave
        for Pittsburgh, pack my things, sleep in alleys

to find her, cradle and reveal to her
    that I would take her away, cure it myself,
        make all the sacrifices one does for

that kind of love. But I just stared at them
    each day, tacked them on different walls,
        drew her posing under a willow, hands

at her sides, a smile I could never perfect
    with a pen. That summer I brought them
        to Manassas, visiting Derek, who moved there

years before. His brother Chris, fresh out of a facility
    for troubled teens, smoked us up each day,
        the pot sneaking up on everyone hidden

in the cul de sac at the end of their avenue,
    where we'd pick cicada shells off trees, admire
        or crush them, skins crumbling to ash

between our fingers. One day they rooted
    through their mother's nightstand, found
        her diary and read out loud. I was too young

to be embarrassed, and said nothing. Later,
    at the top of the stairs, both brothers confronted her:
        Who's Brad? Does dad know about your affair?

Before I could even move, their father
    grabbed Derek by the collar, threw him
        into a lamp before slamming him against a wall.

*How could you say all this in front of someone who
    isn't a part of this family?* To that summer of cicada
        hymns, to the beginning of the end of love,

that slow dissolve within the home,
    and to the still body in the arms of others
        who will close their eyes at the song's closing notes.

Poem to Jess in Maine in the Song of Great Black-Backed Gulls

Yesterday you told me the flock of sheep
                chased your car to the carriage house,

        and if while opening the door a knife
                    was pressed to your gut, you'd become

paralyzed, unable to call for help. But the sheep
                made you forget such thoughts—

        hoped flesh and rinds from cantaloupes
                    and oranges you chucked would land

inches from their mouths, and I can see you
                admiring their bleats and collective trample

        closing on your windows like a murderer's breath—
                    all before your coughing and trembling,

waking from the wave squall and snow-blind,
                one you'd have otherwise seen had you not

        been retching all night from bad clams. Jess,
                    you told me if sheep fall on their sides

they can live just a few more days without
                our help—muscles tighten and blood

        won't flow, and so their dying comes more slowly
                    than a blade pressed to each of our throats.

I'll admit, I don't know much at all about Great
                Black-Backed Gulls or their habits, but before

        you flipped the lights on at 4 A.M., I'd like to believe
                    that as you glimpsed their flocked wings

from the whipped beams of the lighthouse,
                I woke hoping the waves destined to shroud

that stretch of coast would break before the crash,
        finally fade, and let me have my way with you.

Deleted Scene: Before the News

Before the shrill cell phone buzz, the stalled swell of traffic
hazed in summer's early heat wave—bumper to bumper, sweat

resting in the nape of your neck—you tell me the man
aimed toward his face, the slim bullet just piercing

his brain, inducing those screams you never thought possible:
everyone wishing it would end successfully. In the E.R.

they pumped him full of morphine, moans echoing, faces
twisted into paralysis: patients and physician assistants,

children and parents in the waiting room, even doctors
puzzled and fumbling. Weeks before, remembering H.I.V.

can burrow for years, you asked how many men the women
I slept with had before me. And today, hours after the screams

careened through the hallways, the nurse administered
your swab-drag spit test, admiring your nervousness. *Hold on,*

you say, *under a tunnel.* Then the static building, the soft click
before the phone turns to silence: the counting about to start.

After You've Gone

Because hair will not grow slowly as fingernails

      yours is found everywhere: blowing into streets,

onto bus station benches, stranded on blouses

      in downtown shops, drifting into tulip glasses

in fine restaurants, through car windows, and snared

      in spider webs between rusted mailboxes.

We all shed skin, constantly renewing

      our plot among the living, while your waning

you refuse, never waiting, always yearning

      to stretch your arms like pretzel dough, your legs

like rubber bands: hair the equivalent of spun flax,

      gold straw, wheat whittled until it grows so fine

it drifts like pollen through the air: swatted,

      brushed off clumsily, and always swept away.

All the Sighs of Fire

Teacher Impregnates 12 year-old
Sentenced to 16 years – December 16th, 2002

This would be an insignificant flash on screen, glimpsed
　　as you pass the stunned time watching the trial
　　　　on television. Only I've known Bill for almost all my life,

and though some say the punishment fits, my first instinct
　　was confusion: premature baldness, captured face, wraithlike
　　　　glare. Most of his family are teachers, surname now ruined:

scorned glances, unsaid threats, thoughts of what everyone
　　says in this town: newly breaking, collapsed bars, churches,
　　　　a few drunks you knew by name. Now on its way

to ruins: talks of embezzlement, the borough manager
　　who skipped town, flew to Chicago, never coming back.
　　　　A town so small every secret's unearthed in time—

a brand even penance can't rectify. Bill confessed
　　the morsel everyone figured would come out: *I loved her.*
　　　　She was twelve—gradually bursting with his child, age

of a schoolgirl without her first kiss, a boy's hand to brush
　　a lock of hair from her innocent eyes. But I ask
　　　　if there were any small expressions of love, any kissing

to still their bodies or leave them—backseat of a Coupe
　　in the school parking lot—denying the scene scored
　　　　in both their minds of other teachers, home

with their husbands or wives, everything legal and true:
　　long caresses or a few fleeting moments before sleep.
　　　　That occurred to neither, I imagine—nothing but the softness

he felt on his face, the unshaven silhouette of a man on hers,
　　Bill confused and wanting more, if she knew what *more*
　　　　really meant. But are we so scathed to believe

there was nothing real between those two bodies that bare
　　fall day, acetylene dusk looming above front lawns? It may
　　　　be sinful to think of such things, or easy to dispel them

as glorified rape at noon. Because one thinks of nothing
    like that dusk, the wind jarring the car before flecked rain
        slaps the roof, both of them glaring out for an instant,

returning again in some form of gauzy affection. Bill pled
    guilty to four counts of rape. A revelation: the math involved,
        and yet locked simply within a sentence, that of speech,

of prison: not man and woman, nor teacher and student,
    but only that feigned level of touch, the groping
        of a premature hand. And the palmed grip of a newborn

holding on through choking air, blankness slowly
    glaring back—the earth now set to swallow
        what it came for. He said he *did not have the strength* to stop.

Unbelievable Truth: Elegy for Adrienne Shelly

What can we know of the sparrows colliding with the window
that afternoon, her face startled, then blank, insisting

on the rose-stained glass as the cause—though too busy to witness
dive-bombs toward concrete or flights through rafters, too far above

to see their bodies plunging stories below her eyes. Then the hammers,
curses in another language, one she couldn't place,

and the grace of the brash tongue-clicks before his thrashing
against busted pipes and too-thin ceilings. I'd like to imagine

she walked down to check, knocking gently, her face wrought
to the beauty of any woman who's reached half her life, asking

cautiously that he attempt to quiet down, work later when she was away
with her family, after starting her car in the frigid dusk, footsteps echoing

in her ears off the sidewalks. *What was said?* Was that face—
amidst other tenants making love, sleeping in, their longing hidden

from everyone else—punched by accident, or from one small fit
of anger, dropping her cold on the floor? How can words

carry in another language, in one's mind who stares at the face
of a body more like a ghost's, even with her hair mussed, spit flying

from her choked, beautiful voice? *What was said?* Translate it for me
and I'll try not to continue, wonder how he twisted the bed sheet,

if she died from one fist to temple, and how I—if his footprint's not
left planted on the floor—could make none of this exist in the first place.

Prayer: 3200 Hanover Avenue

Bless the arm of the hand of the fingers soon to put the metal
            to his chest, fingertips stretching over the counter,
their slips and misses, bless the smeared windows, the shades

            within reach, bless the method of it all, radio between
stations, static flips to thinner voices, bless your work boots
            and their echoes above, the microwave's hum and ring

through the ceiling, years-passed and caked-on rain, bless the fire
            escape and faces jarred from sleep, soles down the steps,
your eyes toward lovers from doors onto balconies, bless

            your fingers for dialing, hands for their holding,
your voice for its speaking, legs for their shaking, bless
            the rest in your building, hands gripped around phones

and their mouths, and bless the minutes, the wait, the wait
            still passing, split-crack of the barrel, the one
empty shell, bless the snap of the gurney into place, bless

            the whiteness, his shrouded body, bless the police tape
rolled to unroll again, the wheels as they move once more,
            bless the arm and the hand, the fingers, that metal.

Lost Nostalgia: Elegy for Joe Bolton

Leave us, now, in the swelter of summer dusk and sweat
sliding down a gin glass: the same you held in your hands

the night of the party, balcony off a cheap apartment—
voyeur among the college crowd, falling in love with the woman

across the street. Whether I imagine you in Houston or Cadiz,
when I drive through Richmond I can sometimes see you gazing

toward any woman, no matter how far away, who crosses
your path. This is no excuse for you. I've heard the rumors:

Hawaiian-print shirt, barrel cold in your mouth and in front
of your lover. That you planned it from the start, your life

toward a slower descent you couldn't have predicted or cured.
Now the anger, the scoffing at any defense: every woman

was too much, you knew the world would end the instant
you pulled the trigger. I can't tell you this for sure,

but I feel I know the woman in Breckenridge already
(despite how much you feigned to turn it into poetry),

two women hugging before departure and your obsession
with their destination, the hundreds in cheap hotel rooms,

and one who had fifty men before you, before ravishment,
before the thin rattle of the air conditioner near dawn

cooling both of your bodies in the thick summer heat.
And sometimes I think you're better off, as I speak

about the end coming sooner than later, and imagine
your lines echoing the song about bodies remembering

each other: how there is nothing that is not beautiful,
nothing that will last. My book is falling apart like these words.

Watching Youngstown

The chopper's scanning fields and woods beside me
for someone escaped—mentally unstable

or a murderer I'll never know. I make it outside
as the snow keeps drifting down, beating soundlessly

its precise, pale fire.
                          Stomach flu and wrist-thick
knots curling through the gut—whirled blades

still seething over the house like hawks soaring,
methodically plotting the best route to a field mouse.

Back inside: skewed mug shots on television,
local Youngstown news: raped girlfriend, duplex

cored from arson, a son shooting his mother. Stories
always the same: pummel and discharge, strangle

and blood clot. And while I'm lying flat, willing each deep
breath, I forget the process:
                          How do you escape a home in flames?

Poem Ending with a Hundred Year-Old House on Fire

Allegheny College, Meadville, Pennsylvania

This is not how it ends: lead paint scorched and flaking
off the panes, painted-shut windows gone to ash before the path

of a broken black sidewalk littered with beer bottles,
plastic fifths, in the town where Budd Dwyer walked
drunk those mornings in 1958, watched the Western Pennsylvania

leaves turn and shrivel before his eyes, the girls stumbling
from the SAE house in those hours when, once, as he glared

toward its attic window, a girl and her boyfriend argued—
fingers jerking in each other's faces before his fist
connected and she collapsed, the black spreading

toward the edge of Budd's eyes, the wonder of why
he couldn't leave the scene, so Budd watched:

the guy standing motionless, stunned at how slowly she raised
herself from the wood floor. But truly Budd couldn't know
he'd remember this as he scrawled the suicide note

to his wife—how he never ever hit her, and would come back
from the hell he was burning in to kill anyone who would try—

or that the house he lived in then would be ash fifty years later:
faulty wiring, spark in the basement, the cause of Ray's death uncertain
or unsaid. It begins with Budd because it's easier to imagine him

black and white and frightened on TV screens in Blooming Valley
that morning in 1987, the state-wide snowstorm enough

to cancel almost every school, parents and children
staring as he pulls his hand from inside the envelope—
Stay away, this thing will hurt someone—before the cries

and tightened throats, gasps of his name before his head
snaps back, blood pouring like water from his mouth.

27

Budd was not black and white in Meadville, his hands weren't
trembling, and the house that burned almost six years ago
still had, in the late 50s, some care given to it: replacement panes

from hurled bricks, waxed floors, ant killer in the cracks
of its entrances. But that was before Ray burned there—

before the firemen came too late. And as the neighbors gathered,
I laughed in the Penny Bar at everyone holding their breath
over possibilities: Ray dropped off and left alone, smoke

blanketing, his hands gripping the door, fingers slipping
from the metal knob. Because no one dies in a fire. No one

who climbs the stairs on his own, stumbles and collapses
toward his bed before he sleeps. All of it before the nervousness
of the girl that night who I wanted but couldn't love,

as we gathered around the jukebox, its awful songs
blaring on that Saturday nearly all came out alive.

~

Her roommates were asleep as we felt for lights
along the living room walls. Eventually she left me there,
turning and drunk while the sun rose. When she woke me

it was dawn: *Ray didn't make it. I'd ask you to stay,
but once they wake up you won't want to be here.* I couldn't think—

walked across the street to my room, tried to fall asleep.
This should be how it ends, I know, but Ray's face glares out
from the *USA Today* front page, and like Budd's panic

ending with a town in mourning, there are too many reports
of college fires from decrepit houses: airbrushed photos

of the dead, house frames in ash (or, somehow, captured
burning), fire chiefs unwilling to comment, landlords
not going to jail. And the fathers who built that house, who also

loved their wives—and the fathers who sat on porches waiting
for their daughters to return, their sons still awake at dawn—

are gone now too, and I will say a prayer for this: for the ash
of the body and foundation, and for the water beneath us
surging toward the wreckage of our lives.

II.

About Ravishment

To stand for the way our minds work, or *To show us how the world will end—*
　　　　we say what we will, and no one will question

the words. The last scene of *Bad Timing* shows Linden precisely
　　　　scissoring lingerie shrouding Milena's body
before he straddles her, muttering and plunging himself

　　　　toward the depths of her heart, a final depravity
he can't claw his way out of. A train halved a boy once, and I thought,

　　　　Ravishment: sun flared at his back, whistle drowning
headphones, lead singers now dead from heroin, their own tracks
　　　　opened mouths around veins. Imagined rumors: *He was so full*

of medication the train was an angel propelling him toward the sun.
　　　　And always because of a girl: *Messed with his head for good.*

　　　　　　　　　　　～

We don't know how long the wheels squealed, a child's cochlea
　　　　rattling in a black car seat, a prayer sent below from the clouds:
Daughter, let my throat open wide and swallow your light. And at fourteen

　　　　it was Jessica, girls bawling in front of our homeroom:
A sewing circle, boys joked, before we knew of the shot, body slack

　　　　in the back of her closet. More rumors: *She was pregnant,* or *He beat her*
until she had to do it. There was no note. We never found out why.
　　　　Weeks ago my lover's father, an embalmer, told me how cold

her body was: another girl, seventeen, strangled with a coat hanger.
　　　　Over warm beer with ice clinking in the glass, he tells me *I'm humbled.*

　　　　　　　　　　　～

Have to be. I can't explain that I can't be. *Booted over a 30-dollar*
　　　　cell phone bill, ran away with a 25 year-old, stabbed by a drug dealer
before he strangled her. I wanted to ask him if she was beautiful,

if he looked away from her eyes. *Ravishment,* one could say—
She dangled off bridges too long, walked along the river's unbelieving edge.

~

And Linden over Milena, eyes far gone toward
the distances of planets, four pupils locked in the dark. *Tell me,*
        the detective says, *about ravishment.* After the hospital,

blood from her mouth and ears, forceps spreading every rift
        in her body, the end leaves a long, thin scar on her neck.

And somewhere she's alive, walking among great crowds, her name
        untouched, unlike the wings hovering over me, featureless
in their world now beyond reach, beyond vision and caving in,

        trapped bodies writhing until they become
only one: plummeting so far down it cannot be pulled back.

Dual Portraits: Sam Cooke

I. *Live at the Harlem Square Club, 1963*

Whenever they tell you anything about your lady, go home
and if she's sleepin', go home and wake her up, and wipe

that sleep from her eyes, and look her dead in the eye and
tell her... Is everybody in favor of gettin' romantic? he asks

after speaking of the fellas. Live albums are usually bunk:
deadened mics, drummer off-beat, guitars squalling feedback

too close to the amp—always some excuse. But here,
by the chain gang, *Feelin' it,* or *Lovin' you for sentimental reasons,*

the pace quickens, the crowd howls, fret boards
licked and coiled by deft fingers, before *a young man*

dreamin' of you every cotton pickin' night will soon be webbed-in
and dead, shot by a prostitute in the Hotel Hacienda,

the "Everyone Welcome" sign gleaming below: flash-
bulb pop, stark black and white, jacket sprawled open.

II. *Somebody Have Mercy:* **Photograph of the Body**

Roland Barthes did the same: the Hine photograph,
two retarded children glaring away from the lens,

and the punctum, if I remember correctly, a bandaged boy's
secluded, crippled hand. But this photo's cropped: his torso

leans on a doorway, his head slopes sideways, lulls
toward sleep known only by the gods, one, even with his

gift of fire, Prometheus could never attain: a last attempt
toward song, leaving us with the final, incantatory *Bring it*

on home to me, that ain't all Sam will do for you—I don't want you,
operator, I want my baby. Now, scans of the used gun,

smudged receipts, defendant claims. But still his face
we cannot see: the light pale white on half-closed lids.

Alternate Featurette, *Little Monsters*

Flashlights melt their bodies, render them to clothes:
    trapped children
in their underworld of stairs and portals to everyone's dreams,

    somehow mutated,
somehow in love with the impishness of our world above:
    full of divorce

and broken homes, misplaced love and hand guns,
    somewhere between
oxygen and lungs caving in to dust. They climb up

    through beds,
each homespun void of sleep: mattress outside of a trailer,
    a drunk dying

on a beach chair near dawn, somewhere between sunrise
    and suffocation,
causing trouble by any means. Somewhere between innocent

    and harmful:
peanut butter on the handset, LPs scathed on the phonograph,
    heads shaved

while dreaming. And in loneliness boy meets man, boy controls
    world: *Boy always gets*
what he wants. Or boy meets monster and becomes friends,

    an entrance
to that world below: feasts and arcades, hoards of junk
    to steal and love

and destroy like lives. Angels at the bottom of the master
    staircase—*The one*
that leads up to Boy's room—unmoving in the vacuum below

    their beds. Watching
over everyone: ceramic wings, black doll eyes perpetually glaring.
    The last straw

becomes scaring the baby, before the real boy's wrists shrink,
        before he runs
into night's silence, only the leaves stirring, the air

        beginning to choke.
The final confrontation: Boy in school blazer, face powdered
        almost feminine,

the back of his head missing. He leads this world—of fairies
        whizzing by unnoticed,
of staircases and imminent nightlong mischief—surrounded

        by toys, tanks
and army planes, life-size jack-in-the-boxes. But who gave him
        these gifts,

and for what penance? Whose hand clamped over his mouth before
        undoing the belt,
cortex bashed over and over on the hardwood floor? Where

        did this world
come from, and how did it appear? See the real boy walking in mist
        near the cemetery,

as if the monsters are those below, as if we don't really die,
        but make headlong
for our deepest desires, nothing to watch over us any longer.

Elegy for the Unknown Drummer

Not the octopi assault of Moon or the Zeus chops of Bonham,
        not the fat brush
whispers of Elvin Jones, the robotic flailing of Peart, but another
        dead kid unknown

to the few who will listen, as I am, to the record of crash-rides
        and piccolo triplets,
of swallowed sand and shut eyes: the body swelled under seven
        feet of water

in Buzzards Bay. The past reminds us how poetry can never
        replace house shows:
always quieter than a space filled with fans—bands with boxes
        of colored vinyl

and five t-shirt designs instead of books—and only the projected
        voice, really:
nothing like the singer struggling to hit notes where the pitch
        does something

otherworldly in its spotlight, something separate from the body then.
        I'm truly sick
of elegies, of moonlight and questions, of why and when whoever
        left him in

that body, or if at twenty-three he decided to walk there at midnight
        for a girl he loved
who whispered *water* in a dream. All these thoughts become tiresome
        like the effort

not at these words, and sometimes it's simple to make up everything,
        which is easier now
than listening to each fleeting fill, each snare roll, off-time beat,
        and the guilt

of such a thing: to find and listen after the news, still enthralled
        with each track
as if the drummer will never be buried at the bottom
        of the sea.

Elegy for What Survives Inside the Body

I. July 2005

Guilt unraveling to its end, but there's no such metaphor…
friends on vacation, pink dusk and alcohol clouding

everything in sight. New boyfriend, and a life, for once, in order.
But suddenly she's bawling, tells the entire story, like you do

when your world becomes unfamiliar, hazy bodies lost in black.
It takes six years for the pieces to reveal themselves:

age twenty-two, ending relationship after relationship
as remote dusk, gunmetal sky and night close in.

II. September 2004

Through the flatness of Canton, Ohio, she wishes for hills,
tears of her daughter, as cocaine in a vial, unbalanced, spills

into her lap. Doing close to a hundred, she spots the lights
behind her, faintly hears the sirens above the blasted rap.

All before the charges, the long days in jail, smeared mascara
rendering her face to feigned. On the cot, she remembers

the murky quarry, where naked, and years before,
they'd open backpacks of beer and drink in the stars,

limitless words, bodies crawling toward home at dawn.

III. July 1999

Practicing divers slip through the dark waters of Jaquay Quarry.
One spots a gleam of white waving toward him

from the bottom. Unable to pull it up at first, he swims down
again, cradling a gym bag in his arms before resting it

on nearby rocks. The group gathers by the bag, opens it—
wet suits dripping rings around the baby's body.

IV. March 1999

They're both bundled up. The bag is zipped, weighted with rocks.
No speaking or prayers—only awe and thoughts of the future.

V. May 1998

The county fair's blurred, white lights are not in the recesses
of memory, for they will remember the swings,

the fogged lens, the wind nearly jarring it out of his hand.
And their free hands holding each other's, winding around

and around, as if such force will pull each body
into some other world devoid of flash and colored bulbs.

And they will keep the slow weightlessness
of the Ferris Wheel, the camera's own circles building

toward and repelling off the ground, pointed at their eyes,
kissing, contorted faces, moments that shouldn't be captured

but are, and carefully, even the background: strands
of rambling couples below, gorging on the grilled and fried,

all the transient bliss before morning: rides disassembled,
booths torn down, everything spared near-gleaming at dawn.

Alternate Featurette, *Children Underground*

In Bucharest, in the Piata Victoriei
      between the subway tunnels,
the wash of Aurolac fumes rises
      like the breath of angels
cast from each child's pleading,
      paint-thinner gleaming
wet and silver around their mouths:
      bags huffed and bloated
like fish so far below the ocean's surface
      they glow and disappear
before our eyes, cast upon
      pages of books tucked
into corners where they'll outlive
      each generation: antennae
fading beneath dim yellow lights.
      Here it's hard to imagine who
was once a girl, was once unable
      to strike necks, take fists
to temples, breasts now flat and hidden
      under layers of sweaters
and stolen shirts, voices deep, as if
      the chords let loose, relinquished
saving any last shred of girlhood:
      smile at a boy who berates her
in passing, at a man, who—after begging
      him for money, not bread—
walks toward sunset and never
      looks back. But really, when
is it right to intervene? When Mihai
      gashes wrists with the dull
edge of a blade in the park, camera
      unwavering, passersby glancing
abruptly behind before quickening
      their pace? When Ana takes sharp
kicks to her head, ten year-old screams
      no one could ever hear
again without nightmares? Ask if
      Cristina's still alive and you'll

know the answer. Ask if Macarena
        still floats through the empty
tunnels, and all that's left is thinner
        in her voice: *On this stuff*
you can have all the food you want,
        imagine anything, it's yours.

Elegy Ending with the Voice of Edward Van Dyk

"Dr. Van Dyk was one of the best." – Ron McMullen, President of Alton Memorial Hospital

Quickly the children plummeted from his grasp—
    someone mouths each flawed word after white sheets
        shroud bodies below makeshift tents, as if interred

on the street among gray eyes of every person
    passing. Two small sheets. The third for a man. No more
        suicide note scrawl, as if it's even less important now

for everyone to know why. And who knows how
    they fought? If he accused her of affairs she was finally
        unable to cover. Still his website's accessed: phone number,

education, insurances accepted. In the small photograph, eyes
    rim the frames of his glasses, his mouth a dull *O* and empty:
        eternally waiting. Wish for feigned stock footage: a man gripping

his first son, dragging him to the hotel balcony, the sirens already
    floating around the nebulae of his arresting brain. Thrashing
        and kicking, biting and the letting go—*I love you* or no warning

or *God will take care of us.* What can hide in the mind so long
    that it ends with this audience, this sacrificed blood?
        And the second son, eight years old, confused and destined—

we can't know if there were words or screams, if he floated
    like Icarus before falling toward ocean, hoping angels
        would scoop him into diaphanous nets. Sometimes

I wish I could call the number, listen to his voice
    on that distant machine, magnetic and repeated before the phone
        is purchased again: *You've reached Dr. Edward Van Dyk.* Erase.

The Dog Has Since Come Home

Though the dog came back that night to your home,
    it still says nothing of the world: only that the right spot
        between his eyes can be scratched, making him forget

the other end of the leash, why he howled that night
    in the darkening street. You heard threats from a gang
        as you strolled down the street, before knowing, near dusk,

you wouldn't be going home. The gangs brawled, fists
    thrashing skulls. You yanked the dog's leash just as it felt like
        the end of the world would be tiptoeing toward you. Neither

would you forget. Now, I'm staring at the pink "missing" poster,
    your virgin eyes glaring back at mine, hoping two pairs of eyes
        can cancel each other for good. Did you hate that fight

on the street, thinking: *How hard it is to forget how many*
    lose their way home to the sad condolences of the world—the only option
        pulling tighter on the leash? How loud was the sound

of the leash as it flicked and writhed on the road?
    Did the dog's closing eyes and ravaged scent take in
        that world, or the rankness of sewer under the street?

A field, a garage, an alley: anything can be a home
    if you escape from what you know: forget the laws,
        if any remain, forget what forces controlled the leash

and how the dog was led back home by the clear vision
    of his eyes. Did you fear everything around you in the street—
        the last representation of your world? You should've known

less about this world. And wouldn't we like to forget
    what happened that day in the street? Before he lured you
        did he cut the leash? Did you see the whites of his eyes?

And what, after that, was your definition of home? Now,
    the leash balled up somewhere in your home, we try to forget
        this world, your eyes still flashing: *What happened in the street?*

Star City Abstract: The Last Boy Left in the World

The car ride is long, no one says a word. His parents leave him
        with crackers, a flashlight,
bottles of water. They have no keys, wish they owned this theater,

        the radiance of it,
shadows of magnetic and human voices carried through the air.
        He understands this

is the way it should happen. They smash the glass doors, push him
        into the black
entrance, burned exits, re-board and drill over the shards. The flashlight

        calls upon this last
world he sees: frames of movie stars, red carpets, death and sex on screen,
        lovers kissing, lovers

under white, swimming covers, the reels clicking long after the credits
        are through. The beam
lights the patchwork carpet's rivers of blood, blizzards of snow

        shrouding his body,
a car skidding on black ice at midnight toward a frozen lake before
        breaking through

the now-empty canvas: particles frozen, palette and dreams vanished
        into night's oblivion.
The beam dies. He remembers the stories his parents recited, one where

        a boy was eaten
by snakes as the colors, blurring to a field of pythons, swallowed him whole.
        And the story of a house

built on abandoned tracks, where the train stalled thirty years earlier, until
        its ghost squalled
again on fire, plowing through foundation, the child left alone, his parents

        turning to ash before
molecules. He knows them by heart, and in the darkness, and final credits,
        only those images remain.

Alternate Featurette, *Keane*

Newspaper clipping: his abducted daughter in faded black and white,
       lost six months ago in the bus station's lower level. Purple jacket?
Glittering white scarf? The workers know nothing. People passing
       know nothing, and keep walking. *I haven't seen her*, or feigned
apology: *I'm sorry, no, I'm sorry…* The loudspeaker mingles with voices,

       footsteps inside our heads, reverberating off the walls
before the father's own: *She wanted some candy. Was it purple? How long
       did we talk?* The attendant has no idea, exchanges money
for the ticket. *They took her right in front of me.* Unable to escape
       each image: eyes wide, and like a dream, no sound, mouth agape

before waking in cold sweat. Everywhere you look: businessmen
       toward suburbs for affairs, widows planning cross-country
meetings: everyone a different direction. Finding clues: stray, balled-up
       clippings, torn, soaked jackets and shoes, as if he's close to her captor,
some empty warehouse no one knows. Still the brown bag of cash

       and the same gray sweater, before he buys her a dress, washes
in the mall bathroom, gets a hotel room: *You gotta get some sleep, catch your breath,
       it'll pass*, before kicking in bathroom stalls at the terminal, following
a man to his taxi, wrenching him out: *You have to turn the tables, he knows
       you know, go after him.* Then what we expect: vodka doubles slammed

at a bar: *Turn up the music*, hypnotically moaned, drowning any memory
       he hopes to hold. Before the bolted bathroom door, the woman he meets
at the club: ecstasy in such a small space, and at one point, whether
       intentional or not, she looks directly toward the camera, a sudden world
within a world, before he doesn't pull out, before he wakes near

       a guard rail at dawn, the buses rumbling toward the gray horizon.
Where is his daughter, if she existed at all? Always another door: the woman
       with her own daughter four rooms down. He gives her money
for three more nights. Kira tells time for her homework. Later
       the ice-skating and ski ball, after he picks her up at school, buying

both tickets: *Your mom will be here soon.* As if forever… another nearby
       motel, scoring coke, as the maze inside his head keeps growing—
the station almost silent again near dawn, among the cleaning crew,
       drunks in the corridors, watching the night close in on itself
like the question never answered: *He's here, I know it. He's here.*

Ostinato: Elegy Beginning on New Year's Day

In the early afternoon of January 1st, 2006, The Harveys, a family of four, were found beaten, slashed and bound with electrical cord and tape in the basement of their burning house in the Woodland Heights district of Richmond, Virginia.

Let us say the throat opens with a cadaver's contributory grace,
    welcoming the probe and requisition, demanding oxygen somewhere
        in another world. Let us say in another world there are places

like these we know: houses flush with flowerbeds and fences,
    sky into windows and chalk on the sidewalks. Let us invent paths toward
        the unimaginable: heroes caught off guard, their tongues

cut out. Villains gliding through some other dark door, knives
    and bats in hand, hidden in the shadows, waiting to slash
        and connect with our bones. Let us say if they met God

would punish the earth, that earthquakes would destroy
    even the gnats. Let us say because of our fears we would fall
        soundlessly and alone. Let us repeat the feigned: *The right carotid artery*

burst and a jet of blood shot across the room and hit the wall and ran down.
    McCarthy saw this in his mind: Chigurh, the name sweet and deadly,
        as suicide bombing, swarm of locusts, a conflagration through

the ghost towns of our hearts. Let us admit we are not victorious
    at forgetting that which plays out before us: blood instead of flame,
        unable to cauterize the scene within our minds, all amidst the planning,

the party hats and rainbow streamers. Let us say this developed: two men
    slaying within the open doors. Let us say a lock
        could've stopped it. Let us say stopping time would've stopped it.

Let us say there was no shot of blood: no stream, no flow. No camera
    to capture. No vision after being bound. Let us say the throats opened
        and honey spilled out, slow and translucent in the light streaming

through the basement windows. Let us repeat: their throats were slit,
    minds solely on the villains, sweat gleaming, their eyes not white
        and blank like their ghosts. What they saw, these young girls, was the blade

of a knife slice quickly across their necks. Was there tape over mouths
of the parents? Were they able to scream, only that, with muscles
tied so tight the heart almost burst? And who among them was

the first? Let us hope the parents avoided their daughters' eyes.
Let us hope for no blood in sight as they doused them in gas
and lit. Let us say the cops surrounded the house, their guns

were drawn. Let us say *All shall be well, and all manner of thing shall be well.*
Let us not say it's too hard to imagine saving them, there was
no pain, and honey the thing that spilled from their throats.

Portrait Detail, with Drowning

My name in Latin is river on fire. I wrecked driving
to the mountains at ninety miles an hour after
the child started growing inside her. These mansions

left for dead are where we arrive: garages filled
with rat's nests and paint thinner, basements

of coffee can urns and moth-gorged wool. Places
where fruit draws flies and bleeds through foundation,
where lies are silk threads under throats

until they split, where our thirst is for sweat
on our bodies. We cannot reach these waning nights.

When we collapse through bedsprings worn
from former lovers, glare at family portraits
so blurred by light they crack and crumble

beneath our breath, we'll never wake to morning.
Jackie was assaulted before her throat was slashed.

Emiliana shot her brother, sent his body
to the black lake after she torched the house,
watched the glow spread from floorboards to ceiling.

William climbed the oak to hide from his father
and snapped his neck when the branch gave out.

We've scrawled these stories on mirrors
with the phosphorescence from our palms.
In my next life I want to awaken choking for air,

pummeled until the river erupts from my body.
And the stardust you glimpse from the roads

spiraling into split-second green flash
are the final attempts
to beckon you with our blank mouths.

Alternate Featurette, *Time of the Wolf*

Haneke's setup: grueling before the gun blast from an intruder,
      viewer recoiling
at the scattershot through flesh: the end of the world in no

      uncertain terms.
Let us shield the eyes of our children while their father's lost
      to the hell below,

while the horse whinnies and his throat spews like a fountain,
      camera catching
boots jerked back, blood spattering the lens and slick like rain

      until the scene
moves forward. Lycanthropic horror is what we imagine, only
      it's vagrants who

capture goats surreptitiously, again puncture flesh as sweat
      beads along
their entire bodies. Listen to the daughter of the family, listen

      to the prayer
for her father, the pleas in her letter, which mean, at this
      point, nothing—

and of course, everything. There are the stories of martyrs,
      those who lie
in fire without a sound. Not walkers or masochists, but the silence

      in their throats
when their bodies burn black is the signal, and the boy, after
      thrashing around

the hut, screaming to save his fluttering canary, and after
      he sees everyone
turn on each other, listens all the while in his own silence,

      and when slowly
he strips naked, we imagine Christ is again alive in the soul
      of a child who

knows the secrets of adults after longing, before descent
      into the opposite
of love, and before he says a prayer, lens flaring with light,

      we'll question
the wolves, and if, while rocking to the soft, saving voice
      in the man's

cradled lap, our mouths close and swallow our tongues, camera
      panning through woods,
the unknowable will have a name: *Save us all before it begins.*

Going Home

Greenville, Pennsylvania

Day revealed before the shimmer of broken glass—
      first, down Donation past the high school, aluminum
bleachers where the addict was discovered one morning,
      1993, hospital-frail, arms ribbon-thin, body almost gliding

like seeds with the breeze, ambulance driving away after
      his heart stopped. Now, outside Hempfield Park, black
clouds rift suddenly before smoke finally clears, and only
      once to beg this shred of light, enough to see

the few families still left, running from falling brick, wind-
      swept ash, collapsed floors after lovers danced, times
when post cards weren't traded but hoarded, frayed
      edges locked in the dark, caskets of corrugation, now

in closets burning, for all the closets are burning. Next,
      down Werner, where Katie's house once remained, key
buried under the back porch. Years before, you made love
      on her parent's bed as they pulled in, feet kicking gravel

and tar along the road to escape, hidden by the nearby
      factory, ladders twisted and melting, truck wheels
in flames: all of it devoured. Still you're saying, *This isn't
      happening*, and it's funny sometimes, thinking this is real,

you're supposed to escape it, and so you attempt,
      calling names of your brothers, your mother and father…
Now even the sirens have lessened: blunt whispers before
      faltering, spastic and sputtering in this shrouded light,

everyone hoping to find a way out. Then to Main
      and the shops nearly dust, stairs above The Hub
where everyone was hiding in the 20s, where secret meetings
      gathered through the years as boards rotted and swelled

with nests: birds being born, dying everywhere. Toward
      empty apartments above Jules Tavern, where friends made love
to myriad women in the dark, where you watched them
      those years, each with a running start into the Shenango,

lights above the surface glowing like tar, which it was
        those days next to the garbage dump, summer heat
awakening the dead you've come to know this day.
        And so you ask, *Where are all the people now? The screams*

and muffled cries? Our sins from the past wrecking each world:
        nights they were buried beneath so much bedrock and earth.
Soon there will be nowhere to hide. The house where Ryan
        put a gun to his head is a ghost, and behind it more

funnel clouds just beginning. And if you run home now,
        past the charred prison, the overgrown churchyard lecherous
with leaves, past pocked roads battered by years, the only
        boarded window fronts of the last downtown diner,

you'll arrive again at the house of your childhood, fighting through
        ditch grass, singed fields to broken back windows, edged
like knives. Be careful not to carve your shoulder on the shards.
        Trudge through busted walls, shredded carpet, rotted doors,

toward the basement and the void inside the darkness,
        dust settled on the debris, your undershirt soaked
at the shoulder from blood. And find that here
        there is no past, just this memory, the wreck after you fled.

III.

Service Plaza, Somerset

Already it's past evening: fast foreign languages, scents
        of different skins. Two girls flutter cassette tape reels
by the turnpike's edge: one with a face badly burned, the other
        with a mask shielding her eyes. Staring at both, you stumble

by the entrance toward a woman retching, her daughter cradling
        the walker. You mumble an apology, think, *Today I'll fall*
in love with your daughter. And between the walls: mothballs and sweat,
        ammonia and junk food. Here you wouldn't notice a hand

for the wallet in your pocket, coke snorts behind bathroom stalls,
        or the man who kidnapped the girl in the news: taped and bound
in his back cab. In just minutes, the trucker getting blown by a rest-stop
        hooker will land fifty yards down the ravine, hoping

he'll someday hold a woman and make love again. Washing
        your hands, you wonder how the girls' faces got that way,
if their father torched the house, put one thin bullet in the temple
        of her mother, then peeled away in his pick-up. Who saved them—

if you can call them saved—no one will know. It's dark when the cold
        hits you, the faces abandoned there as headlights blur
into news stories, your life safely out of view, the door's snap
        closing off the world you never knew from the beginning.

Alternate Featurette, *The People Under the Stairs*

Opening whispers: hand-over-mouth or drowning—we can't know
        whose voice beckons
from the world heard through the walls. The card: Fool's body
        burned by the sun, white dog

nipping at his heels by the edge of the cliff, a hobo's sack
        on a stick in hand
as he dances toward the edge, nearly over it, away from the sun
        we imagine, though one turn

and he's burned like Icarus, no ocean or lake for his soul
        to escape. In this transitional
neighborhood: apartments full of sickness, makeshift pallets,
        the only light

fluorescent, skewed in from Quik Stops and skyscrapers, the last
        hint of dusk. In the hallway:
addicts shooting up, rabid dogs poised to attack anything
        with a heartbeat.

In every neighborhood: *Always one house.* We wonder what's
        inside the smeared windows:
ceiling about to cave in, how many hidden rooms, what lies
        within each crawlspace.

The only real girl in white, nearly a ghost, sews dolls, predicting
        each death. Burglars,
insurance salesman, gas company workers: *Other people who saw*
        too much. Before red thread

heart-knots of blood, yarn nooses cinched around necks. Soon enough
        the boy, "Fool," and the robber
are trapped among maze walls, dead flies, the cavern of children
        in the basement—then

unknown—with tongues cut out, ears burned away, eyes flushed
        with acid: all kept
from escaping or screaming for help. For how many generations has this
        gone on? Caches

of collected bills and coins, dynamite-guarded in the event
        of miraculous discovery.
The people under the stairs have flashlights, water, scant food—
        bodies of the murdered—

moan like they're dying, and they are. Still the quest for priceless coins,
        this American Dream
of real gold and cured cancer, of cleansed bodies and intact limbs.
        One has escaped

to within the walls, knows every inch and crevice, which way
        to pull each lever,
how each door can reveal the future. But there are windows
        with unbreakable glass,

steadfast rusted locks. A flicked switch and the house turns black—
        shades drawn over
every shred of light. Finally Fool's escape through the smog-laden night,
        followed by his return

for Alice, the girl who's still real, who must be saved to right
        the world. In just hours
he knows the paths through the maze, is small enough to creep back in,
        save the poor souls

still alive. And if we could believe those coins existed, we would all
        want a part of it:
neighborhoods not torn down, stabbings at an all time low.
        But in our world

the house doesn't explode, and the coins and bills don't billow
        and plummet
like funnel clouds to the ground. Because the boy dies, and the children
        still get kidnapped

before they glimpse or listen to or moan what's forbidden, locked
        under the stairs, hoping
they could put into words: *Don't see or hear or speak evil—*
        it's the only way.

Duet Near the End

All around me your voices of threat
        and the dance,
stray cats treading through bricks and ash,
        this house's tomb
of picture frames, eyes the only thing unharmed
        and burning
through the roof: a scrawled portrait of wings still
        hung on the door:
this child's drawing: a mess of crayon
        and oil paint
as if it told the flame: *not me on these days*
        lacking rain
or too little perfume on our street, when we'll succumb
        to our severed
tongues, rotting bouquets of roses left on every doorstep
        in sight—wings
that begin to beat in song, begin to summon
        shapes of smoke
floating from the windows and colliding
        with fireflies,
confusing the mosquitoes, the sting, the glow pushing
        toward the sky
and pulled back down, undulations through
        the singed drawers
and bedroom trinkets, roses dried and hung
        from the ceiling,
the last frame in a box no one found: two blurred
        bodies, the backs
of their heads mistaken for the silhouettes
        of ghosts, their swell
and fusion for the dark, before the last
        distant train squall.

Meditation at Pymatuning Lake

You've been driving for days, past twisted street signs, trees
                 uprooted, roads pocked and gaping, everything swallowed

              whole by night. But this escape has not been

     earned through mornings when the wind settles
          to a silence even your breath cannot impede.

For weeks your eyes culled shapes: swarming bats, gulped mice

          in hawk teeth, wing beats like flitting eyes in sleep,
              or what you'd like to remember of the nights

     when sleep came easy. Now, on the beach, your headlights shine

          on the water, wheels sinking into sand, the first rays already
gleaming out. A couple startles you, jogging over washed-up shells,

          tracks quickly flooding, sand pounding off heels.

              They do not see you there, waiting, leering—
watching them until, like the dawn, they vanish again,

          fading slowly past the pier, the darkening edges of the lake.

Self-Portrait Ending with the Last Flight of the Body

Nothing living smothered in the rolled hay bales: nothing
        but the sweat I can't feel, back halfway off the tracks and motionless
among weeds. I can't feel my eyes but know they're moving, the body's
        shot for blood roiling my veins, to keep the frost thawed
into a thin pool around me, my eyes clamoring for white light,
        the swell of ambulance, a mouth speaking: *Don't move him, blacked out.*

And I respect these neighbors, though I wonder if I was drowning
        would they pull me out, dive into the ravine, frightening the wrens
gliding its frozen edges, and if they know why summer's heat
        broke from this sudden winter, impeding the stalled flights
of the stalled birds' songs. Now the music: string-swell and downpour
        of timpani heartbeats through the soft skin of my temple,

music of symphonies, traveling through Greece, our eyes toward ruins
        in Delphi, jokes of our bodies flying off cliffs, the heart attack
crippling your mother before you wailed in the Aegean, and the hail
        shrouding us the day we fell in love, it's all blurring together. *My dove—*
how you wished I'd call you those names: *candescence, my blaze, soar*
        for me past weeds and the boxcars, past the burned, skeletal remains of houses

into the singe of my skin. I'm saying this now under the last setting sun
        hoping you hear me. Remember my dream of fallen angels in mansions
left to rot in the middle of fields? How they wished for simple climbs
        toward higher rooms, up winding marble staircases, yearning to run a hand
through a lover's hair? But only phosphorescence, forsaken lives
        in empty rooms. Now my motorcycle whirring near me turns to snow

drifting down on your lashes, while your body turns to ash after rain
        and the news of my death. I won't see the man after me, or a half moon
with the paleness of your neck, the lake house and streams from fireworks,
        salt spray in our eyes, the split-second whip of sand dune
assaulting our skin like wounds never closing, or one of us with cancer
        pining for the other our entire lives. But unlike those angels, I will rise

to call you, crawl from my skin in this pure form of ascension,
        graze your sweat by the curtain-flutter of an open window, a chill of ice
in your bones on the coldest winter, and catch you as you're fainting
        from the sickness I can't fix, eyes I dream of as I die, with a dusk
burnishing itself for the end of my world: the empty house
        without our bed, her crib, the pungency of our singular oils.

Second Floor Fire

The curtains whip from lace to ash

        as the space heater catches

before she has time to think. Obscenities

        for *save me*—staccato chokes

as the carpet streamlines flame

        toward every window and wall.

Bolting up the stairs, would you forget yourself

        and consider loving her more?

The lock won't unlatch as she claws—

        howling before fingertips poke

through the small bottom crack, caught

        and turning blood-ripe, the smoke

now curling back your eyes. Somehow, you think

        this would be easier if you knew her.

Alternate Featurette, *Suspiria*

I like women, especially beautiful ones. If they have a good face and figure, I would much prefer to watch them being murdered than an ugly woman or man. –Dario Argento

Always Argento's hands: black gloves gripped around necks
        of women attempting
to escape, knife through the back or sternum when the killer
        catches up, always
clumsy, methodical, candy-colored light still threshed over wood floors
        of the dance academy.
The drums are unrelenting. The narrator begins and ends without
        a hint of departure.
Then we're left with the heroine, her vision: cloaked figure stumbling
        through woods
at night, the camera slowly panning, then gone: the figure vanished.
        She hails a taxi,
rain streaking lights like phosphorescence of ghosts. And when
        she arrives
at the academy we know something's wrong: stained glass
        casts light onto
otherworldly faces, the rain's so loud you turn the volume to mute.
        Then the music
and slow build: bedroom walls covered in Escher, fish and birds
        in three dimensions
going nowhere. Color as stunning as *The Red Shoes* or *The Umbrellas
        of Cherbourg*, but here
it's knives through spines in place of dancing, screams and pleading
        for orchestral bravado—
where everything's red, pulses throbbing down the empty hallways.
        We will travel through
the story's remains: trilogy unfinished, obsession not with the coven
        but the glass slicing
light, Dario's hands clasped around the victim's throat. And blessed be
        the ugly, the bodily
scarred, blessed be the faces marred from accident or birth: you are safe
        now, among the empty
film set and shattered glass, spilled blood the color of lipstick
        on a lover, before
a voice calls *cut*: the scene played again and again.

Self-Portrait Ending with Slow Fade to Black

To this late toast of misdirected letters, swelled and budding belly,
of lined recipe cards and scrawled directions to Millersville. Jennifer,

you've mailed the *Let's Go Girls!* card to me, the Target and Bed, Bath
and Beyond registries to me, only not in my name. So I have escaped

to Maryland, searching for the bridal shower and womens' names lost
upon my tongue: those I hope to devour, who weep at bell-tongues

striking in the dark, heel tracks flooded by the surf near dusk.
And of course I've hidden myself, locked clumps of my hair

in music boxes, let it drift through the crowds and into your dresses,
crawled up spiral stairs in the dark to gaudy hotel rooms coupled

in strewn silk and lace, throes of flushed cheeks and closed-door moans.
What I really mean is: after the wedding, can-clatter and weeping,

I was there, outside the moonshadow carnations, every flipped switch,
and under the black silhouettes, locking themselves out of the frame.

Maze

After the Photograph by Stephen Roach

Let me begin by saying this is her world:
what she knew then as her space,

> her time, one where earlier a boy cradled
> her head in his arms as she began
> the slip toward her endlessness, one

opening with a model home, the pool
unlit and filled, the lit tips of cigarettes

> the only light to light their bodies, fraying
> silk of their bones, and that when flashlights
> from beyond the hills and dead grass

drew closer, the hands to pull her hair back
disappeared while others dispersed: over fences,

> through the black night and closing heaves
> of breath beyond caution-taped driveways,
> empty miles, and she was there: stumbling

over blankets and empty bottles, naked, her hair
past her waist, when it occurred that near dawn

> she should rest, her entire body like sandpaper,
> searching for someone's face, a hand to let her
> know she was alive, that her sleep would come

soon, that when they found her she would be
still, the hydrangeas wet with dew

> and untouched: air sleeping on air, and so
> it was perfect, and really there was no girl,
> and no party, where the neighbors

weren't jarred from sleep, where the screams
from her lover weren't heard, where

> everyone who scattered through the dark
> became the dark, and she lied there:
> the last hint of light through the clouds.

Portrait Detail, with Yellowjackets

This scene you can't imagine: black rat terrier swarmed, miles
        from the walk you've begun. Tied to a chain
screwed through the ground, someone's left him alone.

        Quick and relentless, they pierce through thick skin
until it appears to no one that he rolled himself
        in honey, cologne: anything sweet for the shroud.

He's too young, too small to yelp like he should: curious
        before howling to paralysis, the hymns
carved into air: one as arpeggio, one hundred as crescendo.

Love Song for the End of the World

After Milosz

On the day the world ends the last bar will be filled
with quick pops and rainbow streamers. Mothers

and whores and fathers and drunks all waiting their turn
for the very last dance. No power, no lights: hands slipping

over the last bottles left, over faces like Braille,
through every hair of every single body.

On the day the world ends
there will only be sounds, it will always be dark,

will be laughter and moaning in the dark. The body
will turn neutral, and love will turn

to tongues deep in glass and mouths.
On the day the world ends bottles tossed high

will plunge back down and smash apart.
In blindness, everyone will revel in what they imagine

their bodies would sound like dropped from a heaven
devoid of bombs and blackout, where they'd collide

and shatter like stars, their light
burnished archaically and infinite.

Those who expected a cloud of smoke
choking towns and cities in the slow burn of its wake

will be disappointed, and those who expected never to love
will be thrilled, and those who were blind like rats at birth

will feel the body and what it's like to wilt under a roof
where glasses will be raised until nothing's left but molecules.

Alternate Featurette, *Zoo*

Two blue lights headed for our eyes on the highway, gauzy parabolas
        inch by inch toward
the end of our lives. . . but it's the opposite, camera tracking
        through a coal mine,
fluorescent helmet lights aglow forever through the darkness:
        how we're trapped

and writhing in our imminent collapse. *Why am I this way?*
        There has to be
a purpose? A horse glares from a trailer, sun opening on a field
        for grazing, dying wheat
and corn near the last day of fall in Enumclaw. *It's just like loving*
        your wife, or your kids—

it's the same thing. Fathers, Aerospace engineers, truck drivers—
        even soldiers from Iraq,
amidst suicide bombers and endless dust, yearning
        for those parties
like blurred orgies you can find in hidden pictures: cheese trays,
        soda and whiskey

and ten-plus bodies nude and waiting, captured by the one
        with the camera. But here
for something beyond, as if the trips to the barn were as common
        as the friendships:
all the NASA footage, political quibbling, margaritas and innocence.
        We were friends

for all those years and suddenly I'm no good, just because I love the horses?
        One shirt on a clothesline
waving towns away from the snowcaps, China Firs looming in the foreground
        miles from Mount Rainier,
still like the seconds before bliss, before the body ruptures inside
        for good. *A lot of times*

they just wanted to come out and see if it's possible. I did summertime barbeques,
        Thanksgiving, Christmas dinner...
The notorious Mr. Hands: implying reach and touch, the endless strands
        of nerves through
the fingers. *There were things in him he didn't want people to know.* Always
        driving toward

the ranch, everyone who came to visit, through backtracked
          dirt roads, Pin Oaks
rimming each ditch, stretching leafless limbs like premonitions.
          Then the blind horse,
Chance, and the close-ups in the blackberry patch: always
          poking his eyes, feeling

his way toward the threshold between ripeness and blood. *It has
          no idea what Tolstoy is
or Keats. You can't discuss the difference between Monet and Picasso. They don't
          exist for their world.*
To a Steadicam: group after a gathering, walking the streets for breakfast
          to the few restaurants

in town, no one sensing what occurred in the barn, after
          the booze, the camaraderie
miles from anyone knowing. *There's no pain, no drugs, no coercion or bondage—
          because these are your friends.*
Then the cop interviewed, an actor, sitting in whiteness: *I could see right down
          in his mouth, a child's, and it*

*was ghostly white, and at that moment—when I was staring into those empty eyes
          and the depths of death—*
all I saw was my own reflection. And what to do as the man dies, Mr. Hands,
          skin shrouding blood
roiling his body, pupils deeper and blacker than night's secrets, those
          we all have, never

revealing to the world. *We knew it was going to happen, but we didn't know when.*
          A helicopter over the ranch,
dirt clouds billowing, yearning for footage of accidental death—buckets
          full of tapes and CDs—
all they thought was hidden. Before Happy Horseman on the beach, staring
          at the ocean, an expatriate

in his own country (you can find real names if you're so inclined). And at last
          the score mimicking a train whistle,
bus under a bridge on its way toward freedom, ending up somewhere
          without a camera, the secrets
filed away before everyone knows, suddenly, and without warning:
          No one finds out… if you live.

Ghost Lights

What about the part where the story ends? It ends
with our bodies like machines. Charred like paper—

singed like leaves. Arms reaching out: Come. Now.
Who says the hands of the dead don't ask us

to go there with them? *Isn't that so sad?* The family
parked, crushed by falling rocks. *They all burned*

to death. I saw it in the papers today. I couldn't find
a word then. I looked. I'm looking at you now. *Yes,*

I said, *and why are you telling me this?* Maybe as I drive
with you I'm remembering her voice: swamp gas

by no swamp, Piezoelectricity. *I didn't believe*
that sort of thing existed, you say. Ball lightning. Mirages.

St. Elmo on Boeing wings. Time-lapsed sheets
roaring from our closets. And before our exit: frail bodies

in their otherworldly paths. Bones dusted years from now—
leaving only their voices: *We've shown you everything.*

NOTES—

"Unbelievable Truth: Elegy for Adrienne Shelly" – At first what was considered a suicide, days later a 19 year-old illegal immigrant construction worker was jailed after confessing to the slaying of the actress, who was left hanging by a bed sheet from a shower rod in the bathroom of her Manhattan office / apartment.

"Poem Ending with a Hundred Year-Old House on Fire" – Budd Dwyer, former Pennsylvania treasurer from 1980 until his death on January 22nd, 1987, attended and graduated from Allegheny College in Meadville, Pennsylvania. In memory of Ray Tricomi.

"About Ravishment" – References the Nicolas Roeg film *Bad Timing* from 1980.

"Dual Portraits: Sam Cooke" – Italics reference lyrics from various songs on the album, *Live at the Harlem Square Club, 1963*.

"Alternate Featurette, *Little Monsters*" – References the film by Richard Alan Greenberg from 1989.

"Elegy for the Unknown Drummer" – In memory of John Pike of the band Ra Ra Riot, whose body was found on June 4th, 2007, after he went missing the previous night.

"Alternate Featurette, *Children Underground*" – References the documentary by Edet Belzberg from 2001.

"Alternate Featurette, *Keane*" – References the film by Lodge Kerrigan from 2004.

"Ostinato: Elegy Beginning on New Year's Day" – The first set of italics references a variation on a passage from Cormac McCarthy's novel, *No Country for Old Men*. The last line of italics in the poem references a variation on the words of Dame Julian of Norwich.

"Alternate Featurette, *Time of the Wolf*" – References the film by Michael Haneke from 2003.

"Alternate Featurette, *The People Under the Stairs*" – References the film by Wes Craven from 1991.

"Self-Portrait Ending with the Last Flight of the Body" – In memory of Michael McGranahan, who died in a motorcycle accident in August of 1987.

"Alternate Featurette, *Suspiria*" – References the film by Dario Argento from 1977.

"Alternate Featurette, *Zoo*" – References the documentary by Robinson Devor from 2007.

Acknowledgments

The author wishes to thank the editors of the following journals, in which these poems previously appeared, sometimes in earlier versions:

American Literary Review: "Alternate Featurette, *Time of the Wolf*"
Another Chicago Magazine: "About Ravishment"
Barn Owl Review: "Alternate Featurette, *Keane*"
Cimarron Review: "Dual Portraits: Sam Cooke"
Copper Nickel: "Alternate Featurette, *The People Under the Stairs*," "Portrait Detail, with Drowning"
Crab Orchard Review: "After You've Gone," "Elegy Ending with Steve Reich's *Music for 18 Musicians*"
Cream City Review: "Poem to Jess in Maine in the Song of Great Black-Backed Gulls"
Diner: "Before the Fires," "Second Floor Fire"
Diode: "The Dog Has Since Come Home," "Elegy Ending with the Voice of Edward Van Dyk"
Eclipse: "Love Song for the End of the World," "Prayer: 3200 Hanover Avenue"
Faultline: "Deleted Scene: Before the News," "Self-Portrait Ending with Slow Fade to Black"
Florida Review: "Duet Near the End"
Flyway: "Going Home"
Fourteen Hills: "Portrait Detail, with Yellowjackets"
Fugue: "Poem Ending with a Hundred Year-Old House on Fire"
Handsome: "Elegy for the Unknown Drummer"
Harpur Palate: "Self-Portrait Ending with the Last Flight of the Body"
Hayden's Ferry Review: "Service Plaza, Somerset"
Hunger Mountain: "Alternate Featurette, *Children Underground*"
Lamination Colony: "Alternate Featurette, *Zoo*"
Makeout Creek: "Lost Nostalgia: Elegy for Joe Bolton"
Ninth Letter: "All the Sighs of Fire"
Pebble Lake Review: "Watching Youngstown"
The Pinch: "Maze"
Redivider: "Alternate Featurette, *Suspiria*,"
River Styx: "Days of 1994"
Saint Ann's Review: "Star City Abstract: The Last Boy Left in the World"
Sonora Review: "Alternate Featurette, *Little Monsters*"
storySouth: "Meditation at Pymatuning Lake"
Third Coast: "Ghost Lights"
Tusculum Review: "Ostinato: Elegy Beginning on New Year's Day," "Unbelievable Truth: Elegy for Adrienne Shelly"
42opus: "Elegy for What Survives Inside the Body," "Two Halves: Elegy for One Summer's Dawn"

Special thanks to Christopher Bakken, Craig Beaven, Blake Butler, Gary L. McDowell, and Corey Spaley.

For those at VCU who helped shape this the most: Gregory Donovan, Nicholas Reading, Jonathan Rice, and David Wojahn.

Finally, this book is dedicated to my wife Jess, my parents Ken and Anne Marie, and my family. Without their support, this book would not have been possible.

About the Author

Keith Montesano was born and raised in Greenville, Pennsylvania. He received his MFA from Virginia Commonwealth University, and currently lives with his wife in New York, where he is a PhD Candidate in English and Creative Writing at Binghamton University.

www.ingramcontent.com/pod-product-compliance
Lightning Source LLC
Chambersburg PA
CBHW022031090426
42739CB00006BA/376